LIFE CHANGE

EMBRACE THE MOMENT. SUSTAIN THE JOURNEY.

AARON COLE

Copyright © 2024 by Aaron Cole

All rights reserved. No portion of this publication may be reproduced, stored in a retrieval system or transmitted in any form or by any means, electronic, mechanical, photocopying, recording or otherwise without written permission from the publisher or author, except as permitted by U.S. copyright law.

Unless otherwise noted, Scripture quotations are taken from The ESV® Bible (The Holy Bible, English Standard Version®). ESV® Text Edition: 2016. Copyright © 2001 by Crossway, a publishing ministry of Good News Publishers. All rights reserved. Scripture quotations marked (NIV) are taken from the Holy Bible, New International Version®, NIV®. Copyright © 1973, 1978, 1984, 2011 by Biblica, Inc.® Used by permission. All rights reserved worldwide. Scripture quotations marked (NKJV) are taken from the Holy Bible, New King James Version®. Copyright © 1982 by Thomas Nelson. Used by permission. All rights reserved. Scripture quotations marked (NLT) are taken from the Holy Bible, New Living Translation, copyright © 1996, 2004, 2015 by Tyndale House Foundation. Used by permission of Tyndale House Publishers, Inc., Carol Stream, Illinois 60188. All rights reserved.

Editing: Sarah Callen
Cover Design: Josh Guilbeau
Typesetting: Sandra Jurca
Author Photo: Daniel Laux

For information about special discounts available for bulk purchases, sales promotions, fund-raising, and educational needs, email lifechangebook@lifechurchwi.com.

ISBN (Print): 9798876880970
ASIN (eBook): B0CSZN9L6N

*To my Life Church Wisconsin family,
who exist to see people
experience life change in Jesus.*

Table of Contents

INTRODUCTION vii

CHAPTER ONE
    POINT OF DECISION. 1

CHAPTER TWO
    NEXT STEPS 13

CHAPTER THREE
    GATHER 27

CHAPTER FOUR
    GROW 37

CHAPTER FIVE
    GIVE. 49

CHAPTER SIX
    GO. 61

CHAPTER SEVEN
    NEVER STOP. 75

    ACKNOWLEDGMENTS 85
    AUTHOR BIO 87

Introduction

HAVE YOU EVER NOTICED that the gym is packed in January? Year in and year out, the single most popular New Year's resolution is to exercise more. Everyone is back in the gym or at the gym for the first time. Come February 1, gym attendance pretty much gets back to normal. Everyone who made the resolution, bought the workout clothes, and got a gym membership felt good about making the initial decision, but they fell away in the process that followed.

Life change begins as an event, but it unfolds as a process. It starts with a decision, but the steps that follow are crucial to the change.

If you are reading this book, you have most likely made

a decision to follow Jesus. The Bible is clear that it is faith, a decision to trust Jesus and accept His invitation to come into your life, that begins the journey. However, it is the process of walking out your faith decision that makes the life change stick.

Most people understand the basic beginning point of salvation—the sinner's prayer, bowing your head, closing your eyes, raising your hand, or responding in some way. And I love that part of it! But it is imperative that you know that this wonderful moment is just the beginning. There is a process that follows.

This book is about *the* moment and the many moments thereafter.

Before we get into the specifics about what you can expect with this promised "life change," I want first to tell you a few things you need to know about change: change is never comfortable, change involves loss, and change has no expiration date.

CHANGE IS NEVER COMFORTABLE

One thing that you need to know about me is that I love to eat. I love restaurants. I love looking at menus. Appetizers, the main course, desserts—I love the entire experience. My therapist hasn't explicitly told me this, but I'm convinced that a lot of this came from growing up in a conservative church where you couldn't drink, smoke, chew, or date girls that do. So, food was my vice of choice. Plus, I grew up in the dirty South. While some might consider southern cuisine somewhat unsophisticated, I would argue the opposite. You've got everything from beans and ham hock to the delicious filet mignon or a nice steak roast. What's unsophisticated about ham hock?

As you can imagine, this love for food has created a problem for me. On this side of eternity, weight is always going to be something I struggle with.

In my twenties, I even went to my doctor to see if I had a thyroid issue. I was running and working out, but I was only gaining weight. What's the problem, doc? After answering a bunch of questions about my eating habits, my doctor looked at me and gave it to me straight: "Aaron, you're eating upwards of 6,000 calories a day. You could live on a treadmill and you're not going to burn all that off."

It took some years for that sage advice to sink in, but I began to make some changes. Besides getting a new doctor who would be nice to me, I sat down and did some math. Basically, I had to expend more calories than I was taking in. Translation: I had to eat less and work out more.

I wish change were easy! I wish I could lose weight while eating whatever I want. But that's just not the way the world works. In fact, change and comfort cannot coexist. Struggle produces strength. Whatever way you frame it, the truth is that change is hard. It's a lot easier just to stay the same. But that's not what God has in store for you.

Someone once said, "If it doesn't challenge you, it doesn't change you." So, get ready for the challenge. The ride might be uncomfortable, but it's also thrilling.

CHANGE INVOLVES LOSS

True change is going to cost you something. Whether it's eating less food for better health, trading in peace and quiet for a new baby, or taking on more work responsibilities for a significant raise—true change involves some type of loss.

We have a word for this: sacrifice. It's giving up something valuable for the sake of something else regarded as even more valuable.

I have told this to my daughters many times: "You can do anything, but you can't do everything." Saying "Yes" to one thing requires you to say "No" to another. Sometimes the thing you might have to give up is a good thing, but it is always worth it to give up the good for the better.

Jesus said it this way: "For whoever would save his life will lose it" (Matt. 16:25a). Jesus knew that giving up something good would lead to something far better. He continued, saying, "But whoever loses his life for my sake will find it" (Matt. 16:25b).

I don't know what you're going to have to lose in order to gain what God has in store for you. For some, this change might require you to give up old habits and behaviors. For others, this change might ask you to give up some unhealthy friendships. For everyone, God asks us to let go of who we were for who He is making us to be.

True change will most certainly involve loss, but what is gained will be far better.

CHANGE HAS NO EXPIRATION DATE

When I decided to lose weight and get in shape, it wasn't a one-time decision that brought a lifelong solution. I started small, working out thirty minutes a day, three days a week. I began to look at the dreaded calories on labels. I weighed myself regularly. I started keeping a journal of everything I ate. I made a series of small changes then that I still do today with increasing impact.

Now, I work out an hour a day, five days a week on average. For years now, I've eaten the same breakfast every single day, even when I travel: oatmeal and a granola bar. It might seem boring, but I know what my body needs, and I've developed a rhythm that works for me. But if you notice, none of this came down to a single, one-time sweeping decision that changed everything for me. The key is I just didn't quit.

Vince Lombardi, famed coach of the Green Bay Packers, famously told his team, "Gentlemen, we will chase perfection, and we will chase it relentlessly, knowing all the while we can never attain it. But along the way, we shall catch excellence."

I think this is what it means to follow Jesus. We can never *be* Him, but we can strive to be *like* Him. We can never be God, but we were created to image Him well.

Jesus is the only one who "is the same yesterday, today, and forever" (Heb. 13:8). Everyone else is changing day by day. The changes might be small. Some changes might not even be recognizable in the moment. But these small changes build up and, after some time, produce magnificent results.

So, my advice to you is to enjoy the journey. Don't plan to arrive any time soon. Take delight in the journey on the way to your intended destination.

In the following chapters, we're going to talk about the point of decision, taking those incredibly important next steps, what it means to gather, grow, give, and go, and how to have an active faith that never stops.

Are you ready? It's not going to be easy, but I can promise you that it'll be worth it.

Get ready for the ride of your life!

CHAPTER ONE
POINT OF DECISION

LET'S FIRST TAKE A STEP BACK to look at what has happened in your life. For you, the moment might have been many years ago, last week, or even earlier today. It was that unforgettable moment when God stepped into your life, turned everything upside down, and set you on a new path.

Maybe you experienced that moment at a youth camp as a teenager. Perhaps you had a life-altering God moment in a worship service at your local church. Maybe you had that annoying Christian friend who wouldn't stop talking to you about Jesus until something finally clicked. I know a lot of people come to this pivotal moment on the other side of some traumatic experience. Whether it was a dramatic event or a casual encounter that sparked this life change, God reached down from Heaven above and saved you.

You might be wondering, "What is it that I need saving from?"

I'm glad you asked.

IN THE BEGINNING

This might shock you, but God's great plan to save you began at the beginning. After all, the beginning is not a bad place to start.

In the opening pages of the Bible, we watch God as He created the heavens and the earth. He then painted the skies, hung the stars, and turned on the light for the very first time. Then, it was time for His crowning achievement—humankind. And in those original humans, and in every human ever since, God gave the incredible power of choice. This power allowed humanity to choose friendship with their Creator, but it also allowed humanity to choose sin and disobedience to God's perfect will.

By Genesis 3, the man and woman had selected disobedience, and it was then that sin flooded into every fabric of creation. As tragic as that moment must have been, it was also beautiful. Just as sin entered the world, so did God's plan of salvation.

The first promise of salvation came in the wake of the

first sin. God spoke to the deceiving serpent, saying: "I will put enmity between you and the woman, and between your offspring and her offspring; he shall bruise your head, and you shall bruise his heel" (Gen. 3:15).

From the Garden of Eden until the birth of Jesus, God had been at work preparing humanity for the coming of Christ. The Gospels, Matthew, Mark, Luke, and John, all tell the story of Jesus in the flesh—born in a manger, lived a sinless life, crucified, and raised to life. A concise presentation of the gospel can be found in John 3:16-17:

> *For God so loved the world, that he gave his only Son, that whoever believes in him should not perish but have eternal life. For God did not send his Son into the world to condemn the world, but in order that the world might be saved through him.*

It cannot be stated any simpler than that. Jesus has always been and will forever be God's plan of salvation. And it's only in and through Jesus that you can experience true and lasting life change.

That's a 30,000-foot view of God's plan of salvation. Let's now zoom in to see how all of this impacts your life today. And before we get to the good news, I've got some bad news for you.

THE BAD NEWS

You're a sinner. I know that doesn't sound nice, but it's true. Don't worry, you're far from alone. I, too, am a sinner, and so is your precious saint of a grandmother. The fact is, we are all sinners, born into a state of sin and in desperate need of a savior.

The Apostle Paul knew sin intimately. Before his moment of salvation, Paul was a persecutor of Christians. While trying his best to keep the *letter* of the Law, he was missing the *heart* of the Law every single day. He even participated in the stoning of Stephen, who would become the first Christian martyr. Paul was there taking part! Not a good look for someone who would go on to write the majority of the New Testament.

Paul, who knew sin like the back of his hand, had this to say about his life, your life, and my life before Christ:

> *And you were dead in the trespasses and sins in which you once walked, following the course of this world, following the prince of the power of the air, the spirit that is now at work in the sons of disobedience—among whom we all once lived in the passions of our flesh, carrying out the desires of the body and the mind, and were by nature children of wrath, like the rest of mankind.*
> (EPH. 2:1-3)

There's a lot to unpack here, but the gist is this: Something is broken inside of you. I'm not suggesting that you are some mass-murdering supervillain, but due to the sin of Adam and Eve, you and I and all of creation are rendered incomplete.

I know it sounds a bit cheesy, but I think this illustration might be helpful. We are all born with a God-shaped hole in our hearts that only God can fill. Until and unless we allow God into our hearts, we spend our lives trying to fill that hole with so many other things. Those things might satisfy for a season, but they will never last because the hole was never theirs to fill in the first place.

I've had theological conversations with people from time to time who have trouble with this idea that we were all born with a sin nature. And I get it; it would be wonderful if we were all born pure and without any problems or inherent issues, but that's just not the case.

When was the last time you stepped into a nursery or daycare? Talk to the parents of a two-year-old. Of course, their baby is beautiful. Of course, their baby is delightful. But there is a reason that one of the favorite words of all toddlers is "Mine!" Before they even knew what Burger King was all about, they adopted its old slogan as their own. "My way. Right away. Now!"

Sin is in our nature, but it's also been our choice.

As Adam and Eve did in the Garden, you, too, chose the fruit. Maybe you were someone who habitually chose selfishness over selflessness. Maybe pride and arrogance were two of your defining characteristics. Maybe you lived a life of addiction or apathy. True, that sin nature was passed down to you from the Garden, but my guess is that there have been a number of occasions where you have willingly chosen your way over God's. As Paul put it, there was once a time when we were all living according to "the passions of our flesh."

We all have our kryptonite. It's different from person to person, but we all have weaknesses and proclivities that we deal with. I'm not trying to be judge and jury here. The older I get, the longer I stand and preach, the less I want to be *that* guy. But the truth is, we all, at one point in time, were "dead in our trespasses and sins." DOA. Unfortunately, that sin caused a separation between holy God and sinful mankind.

The legendary singer-songwriter Johnny Cash put it this way: "How well I have learned that there is no fence to sit on between Heaven and Hell. There is a deep, wide gulf, a chasm, and in that chasm is no place for any man."

That's the bad news. You are a sinner, and you can't do anything about it.

Thankfully, there's good news.

THE GOOD NEWS

You can't do anything to bridge the gap between holy God and sinful man, but Jesus can, and Jesus did.

God enacted His brilliant plan of sending Jesus to Earth

to live a life we couldn't live, to die on the cross in our place and for our sins, and to be raised to life, victorious over sin and death forevermore.

Remember what Paul had to say about you being dead in your trespasses and sins? Thankfully, he wasn't done making his point:

> *But God, being rich in mercy, because of the great love with which he loved us, even when we were dead in our trespasses, made us alive together with Christ—by grace you have been saved…*
> (Eph. 2:4-5)

Two of my favorite words in the Bible are "But God."

Everything's going to hell in a handbasket.
But God.

Everybody's about to lose.
But God.

You don't know where the money's going to come from.
But God.

You don't know how you're going to make it another day.
But God.

You were born with a sin nature that you can't control.
But God.

You were dead in your sins.
But God.

Two thousand years ago, Jesus stepped down out of Heaven and bridged the gap. He spanned the chasm, allowing us to cross over and have a relationship with God the Father. God did 100% of the work required to save you, including giving you the faith to believe.

Paul continues his presentation of the gospel:

For by grace you have been saved through faith.
And this is not your own doing; it is the gift of God,
not a result of works, so that no one may boast.
   (EPH. 2:8-9)

You see, following Jesus is not about behavior modification; it's about soul transformation! It doesn't happen from the outside in; it happens from the inside out! It's not something that you and I can do for God; it's something that God has done for us through Christ Jesus!

This is the reason why self-help is really no help at all when it comes to salvation. It's only by the grace of God that we have been saved.

If you've been saved for a long time, I've got some advice for you: Never forget where God found you. Do you want to make sure that you never become a crusty Christian? Just remember where you came from. After you've been doing this for a while, it's really easy to judge from your point of strength and "armchair quarterback" every choice others make because we forget how bad we were. The longer I follow Christ, the more I try to remind myself there, but for the grace of God, go I.

When I think about my sinfulness in light of God's grace, I can't help but be reminded of the lyrics to one of my favorite hymns:

Amazing grace how sweet the sound
That saved a wretch like me
I once was lost, but now I'm found
Was blind but now I see

IN SUMMARY

You were. But God. By Grace.

That's the gospel. You were dead in your trespasses and sins, but God offered you new life through Christ Jesus, and it was entirely God's free gift of grace.

Your role? "Believe in the Lord Jesus, and you will be saved" (Acts 16:31).

What must you believe in order to be saved? Simply that Jesus is who the Bible says He is—the Son of the living God whose life, death, and resurrection dealt with the problem of sin in a glorious and entirely sufficient way.

And in a moment, God takes up residence in your heart and life and does a work in you that you cannot possibly do in yourself. He changes things in you that you cannot change yourself. He renews your mind. He cleanses your heart. He gives you a peace that you cannot find anywhere else. Salvation is not just fire insurance so that you can escape an eternity in hell. It is the activation of a brand-new life led by God, in service to Christ, and in communion with the Holy Spirit.

Maybe you think, "That sounds too easy." I can assure you it's not. There was a high price to pay. Jesus went to the cross for your sins and mine.

> *God made him who had no sin to be sin for us,*
> *so that in him we might become the righteousness*
> *of God.* (2 COR. 5:21, NIV)

My prayer is that there is someone reading this book who has decided that their moment is now. You believe not only with your head but with your heart. God has already given you the faith to believe. Now? "Confess with your mouth and believe with your heart and you will be saved" (Rom. 10:9).

If you need help with a prayer to solidify this point of decision, feel free to say these words with me:

> *Dear Jesus, I ask you to come into my heart and life*
> *to be my Lord and Savior. I am a sinner, lost in my*

trespasses and sins. I believe that you, Jesus, are my salvation. You are the Son of God, born of a virgin, lived a sinless life, died on the cross for my sins, and rose from the grave, just like the Bible says. I ask for your amazing grace to transform my life and my soul today. In Jesus's name, amen.

CHAPTER TWO
NEXT STEPS

CONGRATULATIONS! You just made the best decision of your life! From this moment forward, everything changes.

Jesus's entire reason for coming to Earth in the first place can be summed up in one simple mission statement:

For the Son of Man came to seek and to save the lost. (LUKE 19:10)

The fact that you made a decision to accept Jesus into your life to change you from the inside out is not only the fulfillment of this mission, but it is the first step to your brand-new life.

So, you might be thinking, "What's the next step? I am saved. Now what? How does my tomorrow change because of the decision I made today?" That's what this chapter is all about.

INSTANTANEOUS AND PROGRESSIVE

You were saved the moment you accepted Jesus into your life. And now, you *are being* saved day by day.

I *was* saved, and I *am being* saved. I *was* regenerated, and I *am being* regenerated. I *was* transformed, and I *am being* transformed.

What does this look like practically? Maybe before Christ, you found yourself exploding in anger or responding with biting sarcasm. Now, in renewing your mind and emotions according to God's Word, you *choose* to respond in a completely different way. Before Christ, you might have lived in a constant state of fear—fear of the future, fear that your past will catch up to you, fear of what might be and what hasn't yet happened. Now, in this new life in Christ, you slowly but surely replace fear with faith, trusting that God is in complete control and He cares for you as a son or daughter.

I live in Wisconsin. People here love three things: the Packers, cheese, and beer. It is exceedingly easy for people up here to become addicted to one (or all three) of those things! It might be tempting to medicate with a cold beer at the end of a hard day at work, to seek comfort through an addictive substance. Scripture tells us, however, that God is the one we should go to for comfort—He is our Comforter.

And please don't think this is simply about changing your behavior! The world often deals first with behavior modification. Do this or don't do this. Sign up for this class or go on this retreat. Add or subtract this from your routine. None of those actions are inherently bad. In fact, many of them might be good and helpful. But God goes a lot deeper than that.

Whereas the world often focuses first on behavior modification, God is about soul transformation. And soul transformation starts in the spirit.

SOUL TRANSFORMATION

Unfortunately, the Holy Spirit is often the overlooked member of the Trinity. God the Father and Jesus get a lot of attention, but the Holy Spirit has often been relegated to the sidelines.

The good news is that the Holy Spirit takes center stage in the ongoing transformation of our souls. Paul says, "You were washed, you were sanctified, you were justified in the name of the Lord Jesus Christ and by the Spirit of our God" (1 Cor. 6:11).

Sanctification is one of those big theological words that would be easy to dismiss, but it's important to dig into to understand better one of the major roles of the Holy Spirit in our lives.

Sanctification refers to both the definitive status and progressive aspects of growing in Christ-likeness. The moment we were saved, the Holy Spirit sanctifies us, setting us apart as holy because of our relationship with Jesus. Every day thereafter, the Holy Spirit continues to develop Christlike character and attributes within us.

The Holy Spirit is constantly at work within us, developing the fruit of the Spirit—love, joy, peace, patience, kindness, goodness, faithfulness, gentleness, and self-control (Gal. 5:22-23). Those are all products of working in concert with the Holy Spirit.

If you are perpetually angry, you can take a class on anger management. That wouldn't be a bad thing. But what does anger management deal with? Your actions. If you do not get to the core of what causes you to erupt in anger, then you will only be medicating the symptoms when you really should be performing surgery on the root cause.

When something is changed at a spiritual level, it directly impacts every other area—it will change the way we think, how we feel, and ultimately what we do.

THE UPSIDE-DOWN KINGDOM

If anything can be said about Jesus, it's that He liked to do things differently. What He taught, the way He taught, and who He taught were all unconventional in first-century Judea. For example, Jesus taught that if you want to be first, you've got to be last (Matt. 20:16). If you want to be served, you must first serve others (Mark 10:43-45). In order to save your life, you must first lose it (Matt. 16:25). This is the way of the upside-down kingdom.

Jesus once told His disciples, "If anyone would come after me, let him deny himself and take up his cross and follow me" (Matt. 16:24).

Crucifixion is a shocking metaphor for discipleship, but it's a clear one. You've made a decision to follow Jesus. Now, you have to die to self. You have to take up your cross daily so that you might follow Him. It will be uncomfortable at times. It might prove difficult. But you've made this decision to follow Him. Your destiny is ultimately Heaven. Now comes the disciplines. In other words, discipline is what allows your decisions to result in your destiny.

Do you want to lose weight? Great! Now comes the hard part. You've got to apply the disciplines to get to the size you want to be. Do you want to be debt-free? Great! Now, you've got to cut up the credit cards, quit the exorbitant spending, start a cash-based envelope system, and do everything else that financial guru Dave Ramsey tells you to do. Do you want to finish your education and get a degree? Great! Sign up for classes, complete your assignments, make the grades, and do the work so that one day in the future, you can don the cap and gown, walk the line, and receive your diploma.

Every decision must be followed by the appropriate disciplines so that you might reach your intended destiny. And most of the time, these disciplines do not come naturally.

To get you started, I'm suggesting three soul-transforming disciplines that, if you begin to put them into practice, will collectively help you reach your destiny, not only there and then in Heaven someday, but here and now on Earth today.

GET IN THE BOOK

So then faith comes by hearing, and hearing by the word of God. (Rom. 10:17, NKJV)

Hands down, the best way to accelerate your faith and develop a personal relationship with God is to digest the Word of God daily.

In order to read the Bible, you must first get a Bible. I wouldn't dust off the family Bible that's sitting on the coffee table at grandmother's house. As elementary as this might sound, I'd suggest simply finding a Bible in a version that you can read. Not all Bibles sound like they were written in the Middle Ages by some grandiloquent poet.

My personal recommendation is a New Living Translation (NLT), a New Century Version (NCV), or an English Standard

Version (ESV). All three of these translations slightly differ in how they approach the text and the language they use, but all three are easy to read and understand.

After you have a Bible in your hands, it's time to get a Bible reading plan. There is no one-size-fits-all approach to Bible study, but the method I practice is called S.O.A.P.—Scripture, Observation, Application, and Prayer.

Scripture. Read a passage or a chapter. Read a story from the Old Testament or a letter from the New Testament. This isn't a race, and you're not just reading to check it off a checklist. You are engaging with the God of the universe. Try not to randomly open up your Bible, slam your finger down, and start reading there. That can lead to all sorts of problems. Instead, follow a plan. There are many different types of plans available online or through your Bible app.

Observation. Write down what stood out to you about the scriptures you just read. What do you think God is saying through these verses? Did a particular line really catch your attention? Highlight it, underline it, or copy it into your journal.

Application. Personalize what you have read by asking yourself how it applies to your life right now. Make this as specific as possible. How does God's Word change or inform what you previously thought or how you previously acted? Again, write down these reflections.

Prayer. Write out your response to God based on what

you just learned and ask Him to help you apply this truth to your life. You don't have to use big words or follow some formula. Just be open and honest with God.

Your Bible study time might start out as five or 10-minute sessions. Great! In fact, don't start by aiming for an hour of Bible reading. You'd be setting yourself up for failure. Start small and then, over time, let it grow.

TALK TO GOD

Prayer, in its simplest form, is a conversation between you and God.

Prayer is not a monologue; it's a dialogue. You're not just talking into the air in hopes that your words float up to Heaven and into the ear of God. No! Prayer is a conversation between you and your Father in Heaven. You speak, you ask, you pour out your heart, and those prayers don't just stop at the ceiling. 1 John 5:14 says, "if we ask anything according to his will he hears us," and He responds.

Maybe you struggle to know what to say or how to pray. Jesus gave us an incredibly easy-to-follow model in Matthew 6.

> ***Our Father in heaven, hallowed be your name.***
> Begin your prayers with praise. Start by thanking the Lord for all the good things He's done in your life. If you can't think of anything specific because of how bad things are right now, just thank God you have another day to live. Thank Him for the breath in your lungs.

Your kingdom come, your will be done, on earth as it is in heaven.

Next, take some time to align your will with God's will. In every aspect of your life—your marriage, family, work, finances, purpose, calling—pray that God's will would be done.

Give us this day our daily bread...

What are you facing today? Don't worry about tomorrow, it's not here yet. Don't despair about yesterday, it's already come and gone. What do you have on your plate today, and how can you invite God into it? Take a moment to ask God for strength, wisdom, direction, and instruction so you can accomplish your day with success.

And forgive us our debts, as we also have forgiven our debtors.

After you've prayed for today, it's time to repent for the wrong things you did yesterday. Don't hold on to the sins and misdeeds of your past. 1 John 1:9 says, "If we confess our sins, he is faithful and just to forgive us our sins and to cleanse us from all unrighteousness." Don't be ashamed. Don't let condemnation creep in. Confess your sins and trust that He has forgiven you completely.

And lead us not into temptation, but deliver us from evil.

If daily bread is about today and forgiveness is about yesterday, deliverance from evil is about tomorrow. This is simply asking God for continued protection and grace so you don't repeat the same mistakes.

Finally, some versions of the Bible conclude Jesus's prayer with, "For yours is the kingdom and the power and the glory, forever. Amen" (Matt. 6:13b). Begin with praise. End with praise.

Make this a daily discipline. If you miss a day, you miss a day. Get up the next day and try again.

How long should you pray each day? I think it's more about consistency than a set length of time. Start small. A few minutes, at first, is fine. Pick a time of day that works best for you and carve that time out for prayer each and every day. Over time, a few minutes can turn into ten, and ten minutes can turn into twenty. And before you know it, prayer will become a practice you enjoy rather than endure.

FIND A HOME

One of the most important, soul-enriching things you should do is get connected to a local church. Jesus didn't do life alone, and neither should you.

Not every church is the same. While flavors vary, you'll want to find a church where the Bible is preached. Most church websites have a Statement of Faith that will help inform you about their beliefs. Do those beliefs align with the Bible's teachings?

After confirming that the church is a Bible-believing, Jesus-centered, gospel-preaching church, the questions become much easier.

Do you like the church? There are way too many churches for you to end up at one you don't even enjoy going to. In some churches, you'll see suits and ties; in others, you'll see shorts and t-shirts. Some churches sing traditional hymns, while others push the decibel limit with music you might find at a rock concert. There's not one "right way" to do church. Everyone has their preferences. Find a church you like attending.

Does the church meet your needs? This is a practical question with practical answers. How far is the church from your house, and would it be reasonable to make the drive every Sunday? If you have children, are there kids' ministries and youth ministries that they could be a part of? Maybe your job has you working on Sunday mornings, so you need to find a church that meets on Saturday evening or Sunday night.

There are hundreds of thousands of churches in America and likely dozens in your community. Find a church and get plugged in. More on this in the next chapter.

REFLEXIVE HABITS

Have you ever left your house to drive to work, and before you know it, you're already pulling into the parking lot of the office? You don't remember anything about the drive at all, but somehow, almost magically, you ended up where you were headed. You can admit it. I've been there too. My thoughts were somewhere else entirely, and I was on autopilot. It's happened to the best of us.

God has hardwired us to do things automatically. After you do something repetitively, over and over again, it becomes second nature. You don't have to think about blinking. You don't have to think about breathing. These things naturally happen because you've done them so many times.

Disciplines are not, by nature, automatic, but they can become reflexive.

Reading your Bible might, at first, be challenging. You might not naturally be good at praying. Finding a church and getting plugged in might initially require some heavy lifting on your part. However, the more you do it and the more you dig in, the easier it will become.

Every decision begins as a desire. Desires lead to disciplines. And, over time, disciplines become delights. It's a necessary process, and it's one you, unfortunately, cannot skip. But just you watch and see, these spiritual disciplines will gradually shape and mold you into the person God has created and called you to be.

The Apostle Paul knew the importance of discipline: "I discipline my body and keep it under control, lest after preaching to others I myself should be disqualified"

(1 Cor. 9:27). These spiritual disciplines sound like hard work because it *is* hard work! But I guarantee you this: the work is worth it.

CHAPTER THREE

GATHER

IN THE BEGINNING, God addressed man's aloneness before He ever addressed man's sin.

> *Then the Lord God said, "It is not good that the man should be alone..."* (GEN. 2:18A)

Aloneness was and, frankly, still is a major tool in the enemy's arsenal. The enemy of your soul knows that if he can get you alone, away from loved ones and support systems, then he can better infiltrate your thoughts and feelings and manipulate them in any way he sees fit.

Throughout Scripture, God addresses this problem of

aloneness in two primary ways. In the Old Testament, God-worshipers were given a family in the nation and people of Israel. In the New Testament, Christ-followers were given a family in the Church. In the entirety of the Bible, God uses both natural and supernatural families as an effective remedy for aloneness.

FUNKY FAMILY

Family is great... until it's not.

I love my family, but I completely understand how some people dread the holidays because it means spending time with that weird uncle, the vindictive sister, or the utterly unhinged grandfather who spouts increasingly bigoted comments as the years (and his age) progress.

Family can be funky. The same is true with the Church. Church is not perfect because it is filled with imperfect people. And, if you ever find a perfect church, run! Because that church would cease being perfect the moment you join it.

While being a part of a church might not be mandatory, it is absolutely necessary. Again, we were created to do life together. Church is one of the key places where relationships are formed and built. In a church, you help someone else in their spiritual journey, and someone else helps you. You have something someone else needs, and they have something you need.

As iron sharpens iron, so one person sharpens another. (PROV. 27:17, NIV)

Sharpening produces great results, but it doesn't always feel the best. There are times when we won't all agree. That's okay! We will have differences of opinion. That's okay! God, in His sovereignty, works through the myriad of differences in incredible ways.

You can see through the Book of Acts and beyond that, as Christianity is forming, as it's growing and expanding, each individual church looks a bit different than the last. The church looks different in Rome than it does in Ephesus. Different in Thessalonica than in Jerusalem. In each city, you've got different people and different issues, but it's still the Church.

We tell our kids, "Show me your friends, and I'll show you your future." The sentiment is just as true for adults as it is for children. Are you surrounding yourself with people headed in the same direction as you? Where are your important relationships being formed?

Going to a church doesn't make you a Christian. But I can guarantee you this: going to church and being around other Christians can undoubtedly make you a better, stronger, more effective Christian. And, if for no other reason, the Bible gives Christ-followers a clear directive:

> *And let us consider how to stir up one another to love and good works, not neglecting to meet together, as is the habit of some, but encouraging one another, and all the more as you see the Day drawing near.* (HEB. 10:24-25)

BIG C AND LITTLE C

You might have already noticed that sometimes I've capitalized "Church," and sometimes I haven't. That's intentional. There's a slight but important distinction between the Church as the body of Christ and individual churches as local bodies of believers.

The Church as the body of Christ refers to the universal and spiritual fellowship of all believers across time and space, united by their shared faith in Jesus Christ. It emphasizes the interconnectedness of all believers, regardless of geographical or denominational boundaries, and highlights the idea that every individual Christian contributes uniquely to the overall mission and function of the Church as a whole.

On the other hand, local churches represent specific congregations of believers who gather together within a particular geographic location. While the universal Church transcends individual congregations, local churches offer a tangible environment where believers can grow, serve, and impact their immediate communities in more direct and intimate ways. Both concepts are essential in understanding the multifaceted nature of the Church and its purpose in the world.

Continuing with the family metaphor, it might be helpful to think of the Church as your extended family—aunts, uncles, cousins, and grandparents, while your local church is more of your immediate family—brothers, sisters, parents, and children.

The reason why all of this is such a big deal is because the Church is what Jesus died for. The Bible even likens the relationship to that of a marriage where Jesus is the groom and the Church is His bride.

You might attend a tiny church in small-town Arkansas or a mega-church in central California, or you might be a part of a Baptist congregation or a Pentecostal one. None of that matters as much as the fact that you are a part of *the* Church, the Bride of Christ, a part of the family of God that has existed for thousands of years and will exist for millennia more.

WHAT TO EXPECT

While it's true that every church is unique, most Christian churches in America have a number of similarities that you can expect to see when you attend a service. The four similarities I'd like to focus on are worship, preaching, prayer, and community.

Most churches use a significant portion of their service

for praise and worship. Some churches might have a robed choir, others have loud drums and guitars, and some might sing a capella. Music styles are completely subjective, but most churches spend time singing songs in worship to God.

Preaching, another integral component of Christian church services, involves the proclamation and expounding of God's Word, usually delivered by a pastor or minister. This serves to instruct, inspire, and challenge the congregation with biblical teachings, insights, and applications for daily life. Preaching aims to convey God's truth in a clear way while providing an opportunity for believers to deepen their understanding of Scripture and be equipped to live out their faith daily.

Prayer, the third vital component, is a direct line of communication between individuals and God. It allows believers to express their needs, desires, and concerns to God while also offering prayers of thanksgiving and praise. Prayers can be both personal and communal, ranging from silent contemplation to spoken intercession. In the context of a church service, prayers often include the needs of the congregation, the wider community, and the world at large.

Opportunities for community are the fourth and final component of most Christian churches. Depending on the church, this might come in the form of Sunday School, Bible studies, small groups, or any other community-centric experience. These settings are often where some of the most growth takes place and will be explored further in the following chapter.

While churches certainly have a variety of expressions, these four components of worship, preaching, prayer, and community work together to create a holistic church service, providing an environment for spiritual growth, communal worship, and engagement with one another, God's Word, and God's presence.

THREE KEY RELATIONSHIPS

Although you will surely form many important relationships as you begin attending a church and taking part in community, there are three specific types of relationships that everyone should strive to have: an upward relationship, a horizontal relationship, and a downward relationship.

The newer you are to life change, the more important it becomes to have at least one influential upward relationship in your life where you are being mentored by someone else. In the New Testament, we see the Apostle Paul serving as a mentor to the young minister-in-training Timothy. Paul was older than Timothy. Paul had been through some of the struggles and difficulties of life and ministry. So, Paul was able to counsel, instruct, and encourage Timothy along the way. We all need a Paul-like figure in our lives.

Secondly, we should all seek to have horizontal relationships with people who are at or around our same level of growth. A New Testament example of this type of relationship is Paul and Barnabas. They did life and ministry together. In fact, it was Paul and Barnabas who went on the first missionary journey together, taking the gospel of Christ to Asia Minor for the first time. They did not always see eye to eye (see Acts 15:39). Nevertheless, they were still brothers in the Lord. We all need relationships like that.

The third type of relationship we all need is a downward relationship where we become the Paul to someone else's Timothy. This is also depicted in the relationship between Barnabas and his cousin, John Mark. You need someone in your life that you are able to pour into. You need to be able to take what you are learning from your walk with Christ and reinvest that in the life of someone newer to the faith than you are. Now, this might take some time to develop, but fostering a relationship like this is crucial to the spiritual growth of others, and it is vital to your growth as a Christ-follower as well.

No matter where you are on your growth line, you should always have someone above you, someone to the left and right of you, and someone below you. As you're discipled by a mentor, you become stronger in your faith. As you walk alongside other faithful men and women, you become stronger in your faith. And when you put in the hard work of discipling someone else, you inevitably become stronger in your faith.

STRONGER TOGETHER

To be honest, it's a lot easier to be alone. When you're by yourself, you never have to worry about anyone else; you can do whatever you want to do, and no one is there to stop you.

But the truth is this: you are never at your best when you're alone.

You were created to be in community. That's when you are at your strongest. That's when you are at your best. And that's what the Christian church is all about—gathering together for instruction, correction, and encouragement, worship, prayer, and celebration.

Jesus loved the Church so much that He died for it. Why wouldn't we love what Jesus loves? Why wouldn't we give ourselves *to* what Jesus gave His life *for*? Christians have been gathering for thousands of years. Why stop now?

CHAPTER FOUR
GROW

IF SOMETHING IS HEALTHY, it's going to grow. That's just a law of nature. If grass has enough nutrients in the ground, enough water from the air, and enough sunlight, it's going to do what it naturally does. It's going to grow.

Grass is intentional. Weeds, on the other hand, are unintentional. They pop up anywhere and everywhere. Grass is something that has to be developed. Weeds just happen.

God designed and hardwired us so that, like grass, we would be healthy and grow. Physically, emotionally, relationally, and spiritually, God created us to grow in all areas of our lives. This kind of growth, however, must be intentional. When we lack focus and dedication, the gardens of our lives will, slowly but surely, be consumed with unflattering grass-killing weeds.

There are a number of factors that are important when it comes to cultivating a lawn that's bound to be nominated for yard of the month by your beloved HOA. I want to look at two of the most important factors as an illustration of spiritual growth.

The first factor is environment. Healthy soil is at the heart of the equation. You cannot control the rain. You cannot control the sun. But you can control the soil. As a Christ-follower, what are you doing in your life to develop the environment around you? Are you placing yourself in healthy, holy environments that will contribute to the building up of your faith, or are you in places and around people that will lead to the degradation of your faith?

If the first factor for a healthy lawn is environment, the second is seed. Sure, you can plant bluebonnets in Wisconsin, but they likely won't make it past the first winter. There's a reason that bluebonnets are predominantly found much further south of the Mason-Dixon.

Are you planting the right seed in order to get the desired results? What is God trying to develop in you? Be specific. You want to be more like Christ? Great! Now, prayerfully determine the specific things you need to plant in your life so that the end result will be Christlikeness.

Let's look at both of these in turn.

CULTIVATING A HEALTHY SOIL

Your environment matters. Where are you spending your time? Who are you spending your time with? The answer to those two questions tells me a lot about the trajectory of your future.

In the Gospels, there's a famous account of four men bringing their paralytic friend to Jesus to be healed. The room Jesus was teaching in was so full of people that these four guys climbed up onto the roof, cut a hole in the ceiling, and lowered their friend down to Jesus. Scripture says that, because of the faith of these men, Jesus healed the paralytic. We all need these kinds of friends in our lives—men and women who lead us closer to Jesus. Men and women who, when we can't possibly make it on our own, pick us up and carry us.

Most churches offer some type of small group environment where these kinds of relationships can be formed. In my opinion, small groups are, hands down, the best type of environment for effective, lasting spiritual growth. In small groups, you can ask questions, listen to the questions of others, and, who knows, maybe you'll have an answer or two to share from time to time.

True transformation happens in circles, not rows. In a weekend service, you're in a row, connecting with God through worship and receiving from the teaching of the Word, but only so many interpersonal interactions can take place during that hour. In a small group, you're in a circle where life-changing conversations are regularly taking place.

Both are important. Both are necessary.

In the Gospels, we get Jesus teaching in row-like environments with the Sermon on the Mount, the Feeding of the 5,000, and any time Jesus is teaching and preaching in a synagogue. But we also get a picture of the power of the circle when Jesus is doing life with His twelve disciples and when He's sitting around a table sharing a meal with a group of friends.

If you look at the Early Church, there are countless "one another" moments. Romans 12:10 says, "Love one another with brotherly affection. Outdo one another in showing honor." Galatians 6:2 says, "Bear one another's burdens, and so fulfill the law of Christ." 1 Thessalonians 4:18 says, "Therefore encourage one another with these words." These kinds of activities simply cannot happen in a large group setting while you're sitting in a row on a Sunday morning. These moments don't naturally happen between strangers. "One another" moments happen between known and trusted friends developed over time, not in rows, but in circles.

Your environment matters.

PLANTING THE RIGHT SEED

As Christ-followers, we endeavor to be more like Christ. And this doesn't just happen. It is through the intentional, consistent, careful planting of the right seed in your life day after day.

In Galatians 5, the Apostle Paul makes his own horticultural analogy, teaching that the fruit of the Spirit is love, joy, peace, patience, kindness, goodness, faithfulness, gentleness, and self-control. These godly attributes are natural byproducts of a life changed by God. But they don't just all show up the moment after you've been saved! No one instantaneously turns into the most chilled-out, peace-filled person who is consistently cool, calm, and collected. It takes time to cultivate and develop these attributes! But these godly attributes are, indeed, signs of life. They are signs that real growth is taking place.

Planting the right seed begins with self-assessment. It might be helpful to make a list of Christ-like qualities that you find in Scripture. Then, make a list of your qualities. Compare and contrast the two lists. Be honest with yourself. Where are you lacking, and what areas do you need to concentrate on growing? Once you determine one or two areas to focus on, go to the Word, spend time in prayer, and listen to the wise counsel of godly friends. These things feed your soul and, over time, help you to become more like Christ.

There is a time when, as a new believer, you are being fed—someone else is picking up the spoon and feeding you. But there comes a time in your spiritual development when you must pick up the spoon and begin feeding yourself. You don't stop attending services and listening to sermons, but services and sermons move from being the primary way you feed your soul to more of a supporting role in your spiritual growth. Your personal devotions and one-on-one prayer time with the Lord become the principal contributors to your spiritual health.

Ultimately, it's your responsibility to ensure that you are planting the appropriate seed in the garden of your life. And, like natural seed, growth will take time. But with time will come new life and, before you know it, your spiritual garden will be vibrant and full.

TWO SYMBOLIC STEPS

The quickest way to lasting spiritual growth is to follow in the footsteps of Jesus. While this might seem easier said than done, I want to direct your attention to two specific acts of faith that Jesus practiced and commanded of His followers: water baptism and holy communion.

First, we believe that everyone who repents and believes in Christ as Lord and Savior should be baptized in water, declaring to the world that they have died with Christ and that they also have been raised with Him to walk in the newness of life.

For you were buried with Christ when you were baptized. And with him you were raised to new life because you trusted the mighty power of God, who raised Christ from the dead. You were dead because of your sins and because your sinful nature was not yet cut away. Then God made you alive with Christ, for he forgave all our sins. He canceled the record of the charges against us and took it away by nailing it to the cross. (COL. 2:12-14, NLT)

Baptism is a symbol. It does not have the power to save nor wash away our sins; only Jesus can do that. Water baptism is simply an outward expression of an inward decision.

Here is a simple illustration that might help you better understand baptism: A wedding ring is a symbol of the covenant between a husband and a wife. In the same way, baptism is a symbol of our commitment to Christ. Wearing a wedding ring doesn't make you married, and removing it doesn't end your marriage; it is simply the symbol of the commitment you made to each other. Much like a wedding is a formal ceremony where the bride and groom, in front of family and friends, profess their love and commitment to each other publicly, baptism is the public declaration of your faith and your relationship with Jesus.

Maybe you were raised in a tradition where you were baptized as an infant. I don't want to detract from that experience in any way. What that says to me is that you had parents who loved you, loved the Lord, loved their church, and wanted you to have a relationship with Jesus. However, the examples we see in Scripture of baptism are not with children, but adults. And the reason for that is that everybody has to choose for themselves whether or not they will accept and follow Jesus. According to Revelation 3:20, Jesus stands knocking at the door of our hearts, and if we open the door, He will come in. Each of us has a decision to make—will we open the door?

The second action that Christ-followers should practice goes by many names: the Lord's Supper, the Eucharist, and Holy Communion. This is a practice where we eat bread and drink wine or juice as a symbolic remembrance of Christ's suffering and death, and we collectively look forward to His second coming.

For as often as you eat this bread and drink the cup, you proclaim the Lord's death until he comes.
(1 COR. 11:26)

The bread that we eat represents the physical body of Christ. It serves as a reminder of Jesus's humanity, allowing Him to be a perfect sacrifice for the redemption of mankind. Similarly, the cup that we drink represents the blood of Jesus, shed for the forgiveness of sins. It symbolizes the atoning power of Christ's sacrifice, cleansing believers from their sins and granting them eternal life.

When we regularly take communion together, we remember and proclaim the transformative work of Jesus and celebrate the incredible truth that Jesus was broken for us so that we can be fixed by Him.

BECOMING A DISCIPLE

Discipleship is "the condition or situation of being a disciple, a follower, or a student of some philosophy, especially a follower of Christ" (*Dictionary.com*, 2023). In brief, discipleship is the journey of becoming a follower of Jesus. You can't buy discipleship. You don't inherit discipleship. You can't find discipleship lying around somewhere. Discipleship is a journey.

It took three years from Jesus saying to the disciples, "Follow me, and I will make you" (Matt. 4:19) to Jesus leaving the disciples with enough to carry on the message in His absence. Three years of living together, traveling together, sharing meals together, ministering together, and simply doing life together. Imagine how many meaningful discussions they had over dinner. Think about all the lessons taught while walking along the dusty roads in between towns. And the lessons didn't conclude after Jesus left for Heaven. In the months and years to come, the disciples were still being discipled by the Holy Spirit and others.

Discipleship, you see, isn't a destination. But there will come a time after days, weeks, months, and ultimately years, when you suddenly realize, "I have become a disciple of Jesus."

One of the milestones of following Jesus is when other people around you start to recognize the Jesus in you. It was the rulers, elders, and scribes who took note that two of the disciples, Peter and John, though uneducated and ordinary, had been with Jesus (Acts 4:13).

Let's face it: people might not always consider you incredibly intelligent or exceedingly extraordinary, but let it be that when people think of you, they can't help but acknowledge that you have been with Jesus.

COMPLETELY DEPENDENT

God created us for relationship more than achievement. In our world, growth is often about being bigger, faster, and stronger. In the kingdom of God, growth is about reducing yourself so that you become completely dependent upon God alone.

Work on yourself—set goals and strive. Yes, and amen. Just know that it doesn't start there. It all begins with emptying yourself so you might be filled with the Spirit of God. Humble yourself so that God can, in His perfect timing, pick you up, form you into His likeness, and place you exactly where He wants you to be exactly when He wants you to be there. And know that God uses other people to help you along the way.

A vertical relationship with God plus a horizontal relationship with other believers is a true fulfillment of the cross. Lasting growth takes sacrifice. Our task is one of obedience.

> *"If anyone would come after me, let him deny himself and take up his cross and follow me. For whoever would save his life will lose it, but whoever loses his life for my sake will find it."*
> (MATT. 16:24-25)

CHAPTER FIVE

GIVE

THE MOST QUOTED VERSE in the Bible highlights the generosity of our God.

> *"For God so loved the world, that he gave..."*
> (JOHN 3:16A)

Generosity, in fact, is at the very center of the heart of God. He freely gave us the greatest gift anyone could ever receive—salvation through Jesus, His Son. It didn't cost us anything. And it cost Jesus everything. The least we could do in response to the extravagant generosity of God is to be generous in return.

Most people go through life with clenched fists. Whatever I can get in my hands is mine, all mine! Unfortunately, a lot of the time, we can be like toddlers in this regard.

The problem with this kind of clenched-fist mentality is twofold. Number one, when your hand is closed, you cannot fill it with anything new. Number two, when your hand is closed, you're basically saying, "I'm in control. And I've got it from here."

In the Old Testament, Job makes a statement that I think is just as true today as it was then: "The Lord gives, and the Lord takes away, but blessed be the name of the Lord" (Job 1:21). Translation: Nothing we have belongs to us in the first place. Everything we have belongs to God. We simply have a choice: Are we going to be generous like Christ, or are we going to be greedy like a toddler? The choice is up to you.

PALMS UP

My challenge to you is to live your life palms up. What does that mean? Well, go ahead and set this book down and hold out both of your hands, fingers spread, palms towards the ceiling. Do you feel that? There's a light tension in your wrists, a slight straining in your hands. It's a position of surrender. A posture of openness. It's a bit uncomfortable, but it's the right way to live. Trust in the Lord that He is going to fill your hands with whatever He wants, and if there's anything currently in your hands that He desires, it's not yours to keep anyway.

It's much easier to live life palms down. There's no tension there. It's easier to stick your hands in your pockets in order to preserve the things you worked hard for. Just know that in doing so, you will be missing out on what God wants to do in and through you. You might be able to successfully hold on to some of the things you've obtained in life, but you'll miss out on the greater things that God wants to do in your life.

There's nothing wrong with having things. There's just something wrong with things having you.

Do you know how you can keep things from having you? Palms up.

Do you know how you can live a life free from materialism and free for generosity? Palms up.

Do you know how to give God your "Yes" before a question is even asked? Palms up.

So, how do you do that? How do you live a palms-up kind of life? I want to share with you three key areas where we can practice radical generosity: our time, our talent, and our treasure.

TIME

It's been said that a bank statement and a calendar are the clearest representations of what a person values most. Where you spend your money and how you spend your time paints a clear picture of what in life you hold most dear. Not what you say. Not a list you arbitrarily make. Of course, you're going to include God and family on your shortlist. But does your bank statement and calendar reflect that to be true?

Paul once called out a group of believers on their misuse of the time God had given them: "For we hear that some among you walk in idleness, not busy at work, but busybodies" (2 Thess. 3:11). If at the end of the day, you've done a lot of work and are exhausted, but none of the work contributes to an eternal purpose, then ultimately what was the point? Paul's words serve as a reminder that we can't just fill our lives with trifling, needless, useless matters. We must strive to use the time God has given us for things that matter most to God. It's time to focus your time.

Remember the fable we learned as children about the Tortoise and the Hare? The Tortoise starts out slow and methodical, while the Hare sprints forward with reckless abandon. Spoiler alert, but at the end of the race, the Tortoise beats the Hare. Why? Because the Tortoise is focused. The Tortoise is disciplined. The Tortoise is steady. The Hare is here, there, and everywhere. Busy, but ultimately unproductive. Which are you more like?

I hate the phrase, "I'm busy." Everybody's busy! You, like me, probably have no idea where the time has gone. Minutes, hours, and even days, weeks, and months seem to pass by in the blink of an eye, especially as you get older. It's imperative that we get focused and choose to live life not by default but by design. We must be intentional.

I was raised in a family where if the doors of the church were open for a service, we were there. My dad wasn't a pastor, and he wasn't on staff at a church. He was a factory worker. I'll never forget the time when one pastor got really spiritual and started adding extra services, including one on Friday night in the middle of football season. I wanted so badly to be at the football game. The team needed me! But Dad said we're going to church. It's just what we did.

And it used to be a lot more than it is today!

We had Sunday School, Sunday morning service, Sunday night service, and Wednesday night service. There might be a Bible Study at some point during the week, and that's not even to mention the sporadic revival services or camp meetings we'd have throughout the year. *The Wonderful World of Disney* was on every Sunday night at 6:00. I never saw it because I was with my family at church. I hope you're starting to feel bad for me.

The reality for my family was simply that church was important to God, so it would be important for the Coles.

I'm not suggesting that you need to be at your church every single time the doors are open, but I am suggesting that you deliberately prioritize the schedule of your life based on eternal matters that matter to God.

TALENT

You have talents at your disposal that God has given you to use.

And no, I'm not talking about your double-jointedness or your uncanny unicycling skills. The talents I'm referring to are those specific gifts and abilities that God has equipped you with in order to make a difference in the world around you.

In 1 Peter 4:10-11, the Apostle Peter casts a vision for what true community should look like: "As each has received a gift, use it to serve one another, as good stewards of God's varied grace: whoever speaks, as one who speaks oracles of God; whoever serves, as one who serves by the strength that God supplies—in order that in everything God may be glorified through Jesus Christ."

Peter begins his statement with the word "As"—an implied, emphatic declaration that all Christ-followers have received at least one spiritual gift from God. This means there is no one useless in the kingdom of God! And the gifts He has given you are not for your benefit alone; they are for the benefit of others.

God the Gift-giver gave you gifts on purpose for a purpose, and you get to determine if you're going to use them for your purpose or for His.

A great place to use your gifts, talents, and abilities is within various ministries at or through your local church. Whether it's an outreach ministry or a weekend ministry, there's a place for you to serve. Are you a gifted singer or musician? Then, serve on a worship team. Maybe you're great with kids or youth. Student ministries are always looking for more help from qualified individuals. Are you interested in more behind-the-scenes work with technology or systems? There's a place for you, too.

If you don't know what gifts you have, I want to help you. Here are four steps you can take to help discover your God-given gifts: ask yourself, ask others, ask God, and do something.

First, ask yourself. Look inward to evaluate and reflect on what God has given you and where God has placed you.

Secondly, ask others. Close friends and leaders in your life can both encourage you and call out blind spots that you might not even know are there.

Third, ask God. Pray and discover what God has to say about spiritual gifts. There are many different places in the New Testament where you can learn about spiritual gifts (e.g., Eph. 4, Rom. 4, 1 Cor. 12).

Finally, just do something. Serving in any capacity is better than not serving at all. If you just make excuses, you're never going to live the life that God wants you to live. The hardest step is always the first step, so just start doing something.

The amazing thing is that the same God who graciously gave you these gifts will also help you graciously use them.

God's not just going to give you a gift and say, "Good luck!" He's going to walk alongside you and show you how to best use them for the good of others and for His glory.

TREASURE

The Sermon on the Mount is likely the most famous of all of Jesus's teachings. In this collection of insightful instructions, Jesus takes time to address materialism by calling His followers to choose their master—God or wealth.

> *"For where your treasure is, there your heart will be also."* (MATT. 6:21)

The reverse of Jesus's statement is also true. If your treasure isn't in it, your heart isn't in it either. This becomes a real gut check for all of us. Many of us have plans for saving for our kids' college, for retirement, for a down payment on a home, for vacation, but do we have a strategy for giving toward kingdom impact?

The only two things that are eternal are people and God's Word. Everything else will pass away, but people and God's Word will remain. What if, over your lifetime, you had a plan to give a certain amount of money that would impact those two eternal quotients?

Giving of our treasure begins with the biblical principle of the tithe.

Bring the full tithe into the storehouse, that there may be food in my house. And thereby put me to the test, says the Lord of hosts, if I will not open the windows of heaven for you and pour down for you a blessing until there is no more need. (MAL. 3:10)

The Hebrew word for tithe means "a tenth" and is an Old Testament principle with a New Testament application. It's where we give the first 10% of our income to our local church, demonstrating our reliance on God as we participate in empowering the church to actively be the church by helping others.

Cain and Abel, the first two sons of Adam and Eve, both brought offerings to the Lord (Gen. 4:3-5). While God received Abel's offering, He had no regard for Cain's offering. Why? Because Cain gave some while Abel gave his first and best.

The concept is clear: God wants your first and best, not your leftovers.

When we talk about the tithe, we can often erroneously believe that 10% belongs to God and the other 90% belongs to us to do as we please. That can't be further from the truth. News flash: the entire 100% belongs to God!

Psalm 24:1 (NIV) says, "The earth is the Lord's, and everything in it."

When we get this, it changes everything. This reality

frees us from having to obtain all and horde all because none of it belongs to us anyway! We are simply stewards of what God has given us. And we have one decision to make—will we use what God has given us for things that truly, eternally matter?

Tithing is just an act of obedience, giving back to the Lord what is already His. True generosity comes from what you decide to do with the 90% that's left. It's having eyes that see the needs around you and a heart that has the compassion to respond generously to those needs.

If you really want true joy in your life, begin to give. True joy is found in giving. Giving breaks the spirit of greed and materialism and causes you to be more like Christ, who once said, "It is more blessed to give than to receive" (Acts 20:35).

I wonder how much, over my lifetime, I could give to help people come to faith in Jesus. I wonder how much, over our collective lifetimes, we could give to churches, ministries, and mission organizations to get the gospel to more people more quickly. There are only two things that are eternal: people and God's Word. Let's make sure we are using our material wealth to accurately reflect the true heart of God.

THREE PHASES

There are three phases of giving: I have to give, I love to give, and I live to give.

At first, you give of your time, talent, and treasure out of sheer obedience. God's Word says it, so I'm going to do it. That's not a bad place to start with your journey of generosity, but it shouldn't stop there.

There comes a time when discipline turns into delight, and before you know it, you will find yourself loving to give. You see that it works. You see that God blesses generous givers (2 Cor. 9:7). You find that it really is more blessed to give than to receive (Acts 20:35). So, you begin to look for opportunities to serve. Your ears prick up when you hear of a need you can help meet. Your entire mindset changes from "I have to give" to "I get to give."

Finally, you get to a place where you live to give. That's when you sit down with your loved ones, your spouse, or even with your kids, and ask, "How do we give this all away?"

Look, I've met a lot of wealthy people in my lifetime, and I find that many of them are actually unhappy. Somewhere along the line, somebody told them that if they only had more, they would be happy. I've also had the pleasure of meeting wealthy individuals who are some of the most delightful, happy, joy-filled people because they have come to the realization that what they have is not for themselves but for the advancement of the kingdom of God.

If God truly owns the cattle on a thousand hills (Ps. 50:10), why does He need my cow? He doesn't! But I do need the God who owns the cattle on a thousand hills.

God doesn't need your time, talent, and treasure. He's God. He can find another way to accomplish His purposes here on Earth. The beautiful thing is, He's inviting you into this. He's inviting you to take part in His great work, but it's going to require something of you. It's going to require your time, your talent, and your treasure.

CHAPTER SIX

GO

"Go therefore and make disciples of all nations, baptizing them in the name of the Father and of the Son and of the Holy Spirit..." (MATT. 28:19)

THESE WORDS FROM JESUS are coined as the Great Commission and are some of Jesus's last and most important words to His disciples. Jesus was preparing to ascend into Heaven and leave His disciples behind to continue the work He had started. So, He invites them to take part in this globe-spanning mission.

In order to keep the process of life change going, Jesus basically says, "What I've shown you, show others. What

I've taught you, teach others. What I have given to you, go and give to others."

Demonstrated here in the Great Commission and further taught a number of times throughout the New Testament is this undeniable truth: disciples make disciples. What we've learned, we share. What we've experienced, we share. After all, it's only instinctual to share good with others. Right?

If you find an amazing new ice cream shop, you're not going to keep that to yourself. You're going to text a friend and tell them about the double-scoop mint chip special held by the freshly made homemade waffle cone! We instinctively share good with others.

So, when our lives have been radically changed by Jesus, we can't keep that to ourselves. Jesus is sending you a handwritten, personal invitation to take part in what He is doing around the world. And that's one sizable mission because the world is a big place.

You see, everyone has a different "world" to go into. You might go into the world of education or the world of corporate America. Maybe you are a stay-at-home parent, and your world is your family. Or, maybe you're a student, so your world is the school in which you are enrolled. Regardless of *what* your world is, it's important that you find yourself actively, purposely entering that world on mission.

When you pass on to someone else the lessons learned

along the journey, it has a way of making your own life change stick. It takes you back to the fundamentals. It takes you back to old landmarks so that you never forget where you came from. It reminds you of the limitless mercy and grace that God has shown you along the way. And it also serves as a clear testimony to others of what God has done in your life and what He's capable of doing in their lives as well.

EVANGELISM 101

Admittedly, sharing your faith can be an intimidating endeavor. We've seen it done poorly far too many times to count. From the billboard that says "Turn or Burn" to the screaming street corner preacher, evangelism often gets a bad rap. But I want to say this loud and clear: evangelism isn't a four-letter word. We just need a clear picture of what evangelism actually is.

> *And he said to them, "Go into all the world and proclaim the gospel to the whole creation."*
> (MARK 16:15)

God could save people on His own. He's God, after all. But He has elected to, first and foremost, use His people to bring the gospel to all the world. In fact, Paul calls believers "ambassadors for Christ" (2 Cor. 5:20). An ambassador is a representative of something or someone else. We are called to literally stand in as representatives for Christ in the world in which we live.

Our job is not to be "Bible-thumpers." It's not to tell everybody else that they're wrong and you're right; it's simply to live out your faith in such a way that people take notice and say, "There's something different about you. There's a grace about you. There's a love or joy or peace or patience or kindness about you."

We should read and study the Bible, we should memorize Scripture, and we should be prepared to make a defense of our faith (1 Pet. 3:15), but our goal shouldn't be to become the greatest Bible defender. We don't have to act like we have all the answers. Instead, we must live lives that reflect the characteristics and qualities of Jesus. As people take notice, because they inevitably will, we act as witnesses, sharing with others what God has done for us.

In an attempt to make it even less scary and more accessible, here are four tips for effective evangelism.

First, build intentional relationships. It doesn't matter if you're an introvert or an extrovert; do your part to create purposeful friendships with a coworker or another parent at your kid's sports practice. If you don't know your neighbor's name, maybe it's time to go knock on their door and introduce yourself.

Secondly, ask good questions. Seek to understand

someone else before you seek to be understood. Truly take an interest in others.

Third, share personal stories. In a world where there is no absolute truth, the one thing that cuts through the noise is your story. "This is where I was. This is who I was. God showed up. This is who I am now." Jesus calls us to be witnesses. A witness is simply someone who gives personal testimony to what they've seen.

Finally, offer prayer. You'll be amazed at how most people will accept your prayers. They may not believe what you believe, and they may not even believe in the power of prayer, but most people will accept the kindness of the gesture, if nothing else. It doesn't have to be a long prayer; you don't have to speak in some lofty language accompanied by "Thou" and "Art." Simply pray. "God, I just met Mark, and he's struggling. I pray that your peace and your power would be made real to him in such a way that it's undeniable; that it would quiet the storm in his life. In Jesus's name, amen."

Be encouraged. Evangelism doesn't have to be scary because it's less about what we do, and it's more about who we are—just one beggar telling another beggar where to find food.

SALT AND LIGHT

In Matthew 5:13-16, Jesus employed the powerful analogies of salt and light to illuminate the profound impact that

Christians should have within the world. These metaphors, drawn from everyday experiences, unveil essential principles that should guide our role as believers in a spiritually hungering and darkened world.

Salt enhances flavor and preserves. Light dispels darkness and guides.

Salt and light are both good, helpful things, but they must be received in appropriate measures. Too little salt and the food doesn't taste good. Too much salt and the food is no longer palatable. Too little light and you can't see a thing. Too much light and you're blinded.

The call to go doesn't necessarily mean that you have to go door-to-door. You don't have to preach a sermon. You don't have to know every chapter and verse of the Bible. It simply means that you live in your world displaying the love of Jesus, and as the Holy Spirit presents opportunities, you share your personal story of how Jesus changed your life.

Salt and light in appropriate measures.

Sometimes the Holy Spirit will nudge you at just the right time. You'll be in the middle of a conversation and find a natural way to share how God showed up for you. People are often attracted to your strengths, but they identify with your weaknesses. Don't be afraid to acknowledge, "This is where I was. This is who I was. But because of Jesus, this is who I am now." Simply walk through the conversational doors that God opens up and look for opportunities to point to Jesus.

All of this is centered on relationship, not achievement. I'm not trying to have six conversations or ten or twelve. I'm simply in proximity to people while being attentive to what God would lead me to do or say.

If it's based on achievement, it's about how many people I can win to Jesus; it's about notches on the belt. "I'll give you a free meal if you come to church with me." It's transactional. I understand the motivation, I really do. But that's just not the example we get from Jesus.

Life change is about relationship—simply connecting with someone else, human to human, loving them right where they are, not affirming sin but affirming who they are as a child of God who has value and purpose. My responsibility in the equation is not the output. I'm not here to close the deal. My responsibility is simply to go and to love, to be, and to serve.

Salt and light in appropriate measures.

AROUND THE CORNER, AROUND THE WORLD

As Christ-followers, our calling to go into all the world encompasses both the familiar corners of our neighborhoods as well as the distant reaches of the world. Rooted in the compelling message of love, mercy, and grace, we are entrusted with a sacred duty to share the gospel of Christ not only around the corner, where our everyday lives intersect with those of our neighbors, but also around the world, where diverse cultures, languages, and experiences await the transformative power of God's Word. This dual mission beckons us to become vessels of compassion, bridges of understanding, and messengers of hope as we strive to bring the good news of the gospel to all corners of the earth.

Moments before Jesus vacated Earth for Heaven, He commissioned His disciples once more with these words:

> *"But you will receive power when the Holy Spirit has come upon you, and you will be my witnesses in Jerusalem and in all Judea and Samaria, and to the end of the earth."* (ACTS 1:8)

I like to think of these locations as concentric circles that increase in size and scope the further they get from the center. Let's start, as Jesus did, with Jerusalem.

At this time, Jerusalem was basically the epicenter of Jewish society. This is where Jesus was when He gave this commission, and this is where His disciples were operating from when they heard this commission. Your "Jerusalem" is the city in which you live, where you spend the majority of your time, where you work, eat, and play.

Judea and Samaria were the greater regions outside of the city, the proverbial highways and byways. Judea was a vast area that included other cities like Bethlehem and Jericho. Even further north was the region of Samaria that included places like Shechem and Caesarea. Your "Judea and Samaria" could include your state and even your country.

The end of the earth is literally all around the world to people and places both unlike and unfamiliar to Jesus's disciples. In our context, this easily translates to diverse countries and contexts far away from home.

Here in the twenty-first century, we can learn a lot from Jesus's parting directives to His disciples. Primarily, we must understand that our approach to evangelism cannot be either/or, but must be both/and. We do not get to pick and choose.

If we're just concerned about the far reaches of the world, but we're not taking care of our "Jerusalem," then we're not really doing what God's called us to do. We have a responsibility to our neighbor. We have a responsibility to first go into our own "Jerusalem" to show love and compassion to the person down the street or to a coworker in need.

The flip side of that is true, too. Sometimes we have this notion that the world can take care of itself; let's just focus on the here and now. In doing so, we distort the call of Christ and turn Jesus's Great Commission into our Great Comfort.

As Jesus outlined it, the best strategy is to begin where you are, doing what God has called you to do in the culture and context where He's placed you, and then, as God opens doors, expand your influence and reach around the world. Begin in your own backyard and grow from there.

There are some people that are never going to move out of their hometown. That's fine. However, no one is exempt from Jesus's commission to go into all the world. Thankfully, there are a number of ways to fulfill the commission to go.

Most churches provide opportunities for individuals to participate in a short-term mission trip, anywhere from a few days to a couple of weeks, to a foreign country to partner with ministries already there on the ground. This is an excellent way for Christ-followers to step outside their comfort zones, immerse themselves in unfamiliar cultures, and engage in hands-on service opportunities that help believers maintain connectivity to the global body of Christ.

Another way to fulfill the commission to go is to partner with missionaries and missions organizations through financial assistance and prayer. You won't always be able to physically go yourself, but you can support others who are hard at work taking the gospel to the far reaches of the earth. Your church will likely provide many opportunities throughout the year to learn about various needs around the world and to give in missions offerings that directly impact places that you might never go to and people you might never see.

Around the corner, around the world. One is personal evangelism; the other is missions. Though they vary in a number of ways, they have the same motivation of the heart. Luke 12:48 (NKJV) says, "To whom much is given, from him much will be required." In Christ, I've been given so much grace. Therefore, I want to give grace in return. I've experienced so much life change. In return, I want to help bring life change to others, one person at a time.

SHARE YOUR STORY

One surefire way to solidify life change in your own life is to go. In some ways, this is a "Part Two" to baptism. If water baptism was your public declaration of an inward decision, going into the world as a witness is an extenuation of that bold claim.

It was in their going that Jesus's disciples took what was private and made it public. They each had a story they needed to tell. Matthew went from being a tax collector to recording the very first book of the New Testament, breaking the 400 years of silence between the Old Testament and the New. John was a fisherman who had his life changed by Jesus and ended up writing a Gospel of his own. Peter didn't write much but would be prolific in his establishment of the early church in Jerusalem. It's due to the faith and testimony of these disciples that Christianity spread rapidly around the world and is as pervasive as it is today.

Go and share your story of life change. Not only will it impact the lives of the people who hear your story, but it will have an incredible impact on your life as well. Your faith will grow and your relationship with God will strengthen the more you share your story.

And you won't have to travel very far or wait very long to share your story. God has a divine way of bringing people who are in need of life change across our path. You've just got to be open. You've got to have your antenna up so that when the God-ordained encounter takes place, you are ready to share your faith with truth and grace.

Truth is acknowledging the reality that we're all lost in our sins. Grace is the fact that Jesus paid the price for our sins on the cross. Truth shines a light on sins, problems, issues, and inconsistencies. Grace points to God as the source of our strength needed to overcome these obstacles. Truth says, "This is my story." Grace says, "But look at what God has done."

God is inviting you to participate in His mission to save the world. This divine commission transcends barriers of distance, culture, and circumstance, beckoning us to collaborate with the Creator of all things in the grand narrative of salvation. In answering this call, we not only fulfill our purpose as followers of Christ but also join a lineage of disciples who have carried the torch of faith through history.

> For "everyone who calls on the name of the Lord will be saved." How then will they call on him in whom

they have not believed? And how are they to believe in him of whom they have never heard? And how are they to hear without someone preaching? And how are they to preach unless they are sent? As it is written, "How beautiful are the feet of those who preach the good news!" (ROM. 10:13-15)

CHAPTER SEVEN

NEVER STOP

ONE OF MY FAVORITE VERSES in all of Scripture is a word of encouragement from the Apostle Paul in Galatians 6:9: "And let us not grow weary of doing good, for in due season we will reap, if we do not give up."

Oh, how I wish that every Christ-follower could embody this single sentence.

The road of life change is not linear. It doesn't have a beginning point and an ending point. It's not a dash between two dates on a tombstone.

Furthermore, you don't control the way life works. Unexpected things are bound to happen. There will be sickness and death. There will be hardships and complexities:

lost jobs, broken friendships, unanticipated expenditures, seasons of depression and despair, sleepless nights. No one said any of this was going to be easy.

Very few things in life you master. Most things you end up managing.

The good news is that we all deal with this.

The bad news is that we all deal with this.

In most things, you and I only have control over the input. We have some control over some of the variables—the things we say, the plans we make, the actions we take. We do not have control over the outcome. That's where the historic Serenity Prayer comes into play: "God, grant me the serenity to accept the things I cannot change, the courage to change the things I can, and the wisdom to know the difference."

Though you might not have control over what life chooses to throw your way, you do have control over one choice: will you quit, or will you persevere?

PESKY THORNS

Paul talks about having a metaphorical thorn in his flesh (2 Cor. 12:7). He calls it "a messenger of Satan" sent to harass him, to beat him down so that he would never become conceited. Paul pleaded with the Lord multiple times, begging God to remove the affliction. God's response? "My grace is sufficient for you, for my power is made perfect in weakness" (2 Cor. 12:9).

Every single one of us has a proverbial thorn in the flesh. Superman has kryptonite, Achilles has a heel, and you, too, have a weakness that you battle.

As you venture through this life change, it is not uncommon to face issues physically, mentally, spiritually, emotionally, or socially that stick with you for the rest of your life. That's normal. The question isn't, are you struggling with something? We all are. The question isn't, is there something wrong with you? Of course there is, but we're all messed up. The question isn't even, what's the object of my struggle? Your issue might be different than mine, but we all have issues! The question is, are you persevering?

The number of times in my life that I have battled my weight might surprise you. For me, it will always be a weakness because I like to eat, and I don't like to work out. What I've done, though, is I have refused to quit. I have stopped and started again so many times. But the key is refusing to quit doing what is good. In doing so, I have done what many have called "failing forward." With each temporary failure, I've learned another way not to do this.

In his efforts to invent the lightbulb, Thomas Edison said, "I have not failed. I've just found 10,000 ways that won't work."

When you fail, because you inevitably will, fail forward. Every time you fail, learn something new about yourself, about your struggle, about what works and what doesn't, and do your best to implement new strategies the next time you're faced with the same problem.

Thorns are uncomfortable. Thorns sting. Thorns frustrate. But they are not fatal. In fact, in the grand scheme of things, thorns are relatively small nuisances. So, the next time you face a thorn, a struggle, or a setback, don't allow it to paralyze your progress. Learn from your mistakes. Fail forward. Refuse to quit. You will progress with each and every refusal.

MAKING IT TO THE FINISH LINE

This Christian journey isn't a short race. We're not involved in some 100-meter dash. This is more of a marathon that will ultimately meet its conclusion when God takes us home. Yet, even then, our lives will simply begin the next phase of their journey.

> *Not that I have already obtained this or am already perfect, but I press on to make it my own, because Christ Jesus has made me his own. Brothers, I do not consider that I have made it my own. But one thing I do: forgetting what lies behind and straining forward to what lies ahead, I press on toward the goal for the prize of the upward call of God in Christ Jesus.* (PHIL. 3:12-14)

As you run the race of life, are you progressing, or are you digressing? Are you pressing forward, or are you falling back? Are you, like Paul, choosing to forget what lies behind and striving for what lies ahead?

My refusal to quit was sparked in grade school. I was always involved in sports—football in the fall, basketball in the winter, soccer in the spring, and baseball in the summer. There were tryouts, but everybody made it on the team, including yours truly.

On day one, I was ecstatic to put on the gear and run out onto the field. But about three to four weeks into it, I would get tired. I didn't like practicing. I got bored quickly. So, I would quit.

I repeated this for a couple of years until one day in fifth grade. Glorified tryouts were that day and I was letting my nerves show. I distinctly remember one of my friends saying to me, "It doesn't matter how you do. You're gonna quit anyhow because that's what you do. You're a quitter."

Ouch!

There was something about my friend's remark that rooted itself in my prepubescent psyche. That day, I said to myself, "I know I'm not great at a lot of these sports, and I still might not like practicing, but I am going to play every sport, and if it costs me my life, I am not going to quit."

I may not be good. I may not always excel. I won't always

win. I won't always like it. But the one constant is that I'm going to refuse to quit. I will keep running.

That day, I learned one of life's most valuable lessons. I learned the key to life change.

Life change is not about reaching some particular summit. It's about refusing to quit. It's about getting up when you're knocked down. It's about failing forward and treating every failure as a lesson learned. It's about moving forward one step at a time.

You might not be the fastest. You'll have some scraped knees and twisted ankles along the way. From time to time, you'll be out of breath and get a stitch in your side. Just keep running. As long as you keep putting one foot in front of the other, you'll make it to the finish line.

WHEN YOU DON'T FEEL IT

Please understand that most of what's in this book are tools, not rules. It's best not to treat all of these things as some kind of checklist that, as long as you do these things, everything will work out in your favor. You can do every single one of these practices mentioned in the previous chapters, and you will still have days where you just don't feel like it's worth it. There will be days when you wonder if this Christian life is all it's cracked up to be.

My encouragement would be to recognize these feelings for what they are. Don't try to ignore or avoid them.

But do know that, as Christ-followers, we walk by faith, not by emotions. Allow yourself to feel, but remind yourself of what you know.

I find it helpful to speak the Word of God over my feelings.

"Come to me, all who labor and are heavy laden, and I will give you rest. Take my yoke upon you, and learn from me, for I am gentle and lowly in heart, and you will find rest for your souls."
      (MATT. 11:28-29)

"My grace is sufficient for you, for my power is made perfect in weakness." (2 COR. 12:9)

The Lord is my strength and my shield; in him my heart trusts, and I am helped; my heart exults, and with my song I give thanks to him. (PS. 28:7)

But they who wait for the Lord shall renew their strength; they shall mount up with wings like eagles; they shall run and not be weary; they shall walk and not faint. (ISA. 40:31)

There are hundreds of verses throughout Scripture that can help remind your soul of God's goodness and nearness even when you don't feel it.

It's also important to remember that there is no spring without winter.

There will be seasons in life that feel dry, that feel stale. They are inevitable. You just can't stay there. It's called a season for a reason. Seasons come, and seasons go. No season is forever.

What do you do if you're in the middle of a winter season where it seems everything is going wrong and God is nowhere to be found?

First, give yourself permission to acknowledge the season you're in. There's no benefit to closing your eyes, clenching your fists, and acting like everything's okay when everything is definitely not okay.

Secondly, evaluate and identify the issues you're facing. Are they in your control or completely out of your control? How long have you been in this season? If you have difficulty deciphering any of this, it's never a bad thing to seek professional help. What you're dealing with could very well be medical, or mental, or both.

Thirdly, create intentional disruption. Adjust your rhythms. I once heard pastor and author Mark Batterson say, "Change of place plus change of pace equals change of perspective." Maybe your pace is too fast and you need to slow down. Maybe you've spent too much time at the office or at the house and it's past time to resurface for some fresh air. Some combination of changing your place and your pace will lead to a change of perspective. This is a super effective way of getting out of the rut.

Now, please hear me. The above advice is not a checklist that, if you follow, you will immediately leap out of whatever difficult season you're facing into a much more enjoyable one. That's just not how life works. However, these are steps that I've found helpful in my life, and I've seen work in the lives of others as well.

When you feel that your relationship with the Lord has gone stale, go back to the beginning. To an old church that had abandoned their first love, Jesus instructed them to "Remember therefore from where you have fallen; repent, and do the works you did at first" (Rev. 2:5). Repent and go back to the beginning. What were the things that once caused your heart to leap for the things of God? What were the books you read? The prayers you prayed? The songs you worshiped to? Go back to those things. Do those things again so that your heart might once again be set ablaze.

LAST WORDS

Life change is a journey. You might be brand-new to this whole Jesus thing, or you might have been following Jesus for over fifty years; we're all on this road together.

Give your best to the Lord even when it's not awesome. God, in His infinite mercy and grace, has a way of taking your best, redeeming that, and using it for your good and His glory.

What the enemy tries to use to destroy you—your weaknesses, your detours, your frustrations, the times when you crash and burn, the times you want to quit, and the times you do quit but ultimately choose to get back up and reengage, God takes and uses all of those broken pieces to create a beautiful mosaic that ten, twenty, or ten thousand years down the road, you'll be able to look back on to see how God was at work all along.

There's always another chapter.

There's always another struggle, but there's always another victory.

Rest in the fact that you're not enough, but God is. You aren't strong enough or capable enough. You don't have it all figured out. You can't possibly do it on your own. But God. He is strong. He is capable. He has it all figured out. And if you will simply lean into Him time and time again and refuse to give up, refuse to throw in the towel, refuse to quit, God will see you through to the very end.

Acknowledgments

I WANT FIRST TO EXPRESS love and gratitude to my wife, Tammy. You are my greatest partner in life and ministry. Thank you for your unending love and support. I love you.

To my daughters, Ana and Ava: you are my sunshine, God's gift, and the clearest example of the Father's heart on this side of eternity.

To my parents, Jerry and Paula, and my in-laws, Allen and Dixie: thank you for living out this book. I am forever grateful for your godly example and for raising Tammy and me to love and follow Jesus at an early age.

I am incredibly thankful for our Life Church elders and staff. Thank you for your committed leadership to Jesus and for striving daily to bring the gospel around the corner and around the world.

Thank you to Ryan Coggins, my Executive Pastor and friend, who leads Life Church with me "heart and soul." Much love and respect.

Thank you, Dustin Johnston, for making this book a reality. I could not have completed this book without your discipline, hard work, and diligence.

Finally, I aim to live a life of gratitude to the One whom this book is all about—Jesus, the author and finisher of my faith.

Author Bio

DR. AARON COLE is the Senior Pastor of Life Church Wisconsin. He currently serves on multiple boards for various religious, educational, and nonprofit organizations. Most notably, Aaron serves as the Chairman of the Board at Convoy of Hope and on the Board of Trustees at Evangel University. Aaron received his bachelor's degree in Theology from Central Bible College, his Master of Theology degree from Oral Robert's University, and his Doctor of Ministry degree from George Fox University. When he is not in Wisconsin, he travels internationally, supporting missions and teaching leadership for both professionals and pastors. Aaron and his wife, Tammy, have two daughters, Ana and Ava, and just welcomed to the world their very first grandchild, Amelia.